Living With It

Living With It

Marjorie Power

Book Design by George E. Murphy, Jr.
Composition by Coastal Composition, Box 2600, Ocean Bluff, MA 02065

First Edition

Copyright ©1983 by Marjorie Power

Library of Congress Catalog Card Number: 83-050235
ISBN: 0-931694-24-8

Wampeter Press, Box 512, Green Harbor, MA 02041

This book is dedicated to Nelson Bentley.

Grateful acknowledgement is made to the editors of the following magazines in which some of these poems first appeared:

The Archer . . . . *Blossom Shock*

Sequoia . . . . *For A Kinsman*

Puget Soundings . . . . *Primary Colors*

Crab Creek Review . . . . *Through Kitchen Windows*

The Bellingham Review . . . . . *Today*
Living With It
Sticks Equation
Her Transfiguration
Prayer Of My Thirty-Fifth Winter
To A Childhood Friend

CONTENTS

March

Through an alley
winter drags a wake
of window shades
shut to the grey
and to the gusts
pushing the air
as though in birth
and to the holes
in the pavement
where green explodes
My name is March
the only name alive
In the world's wail
the song is mine

Old Lady At The Beauty Shop

There remains no such matter as being on time
She stares the mirror in the eye
tosses years of catered parties
down her back

The hairdresser extracts the brush
from the hands which lead their own life
An outline of the old lady pays and walks out
In the beauty shop are things I can touch

The ex-customer enters her car
unleashing whiteness
from pins and combs
She lets her wheels go as her chauffeur never had

The city drops into her jewel box
The lid lowers
She parks under an oak
The brown leaves close their lips

I can see her
reclining the driver's seat
withdrawing the smile from the light which had been her face
Pray for me she calls and pray for God

Laundry

Into this pile have crept certain fabrics
with no idea what the word earth means
Their heritage dates back to yesterday
Yesterday night they shattered
In three days they will rise again
in a new form promising to hide stains for good

Hurrying through the forest are humans clutching birthday gifts
The humans murmur Animals Animals lend us your fur
Shall we lift up our eyes they wonder
wondering where to ask this question
and sometimes what the question is
that waits behind it

while they drop these uncertainties one by one
into a laundry basket overflowing
with the only reply it has

Letterhead

It is coming for me
writing paper with my name
and the present location of my tightrope

The elephant dangles from its trunk and why not?
it has always wanted to be an ape
The bears are selling drinks
to pay their way to town
Another liontamer was shot but he'll live
Civilization is running high See the trapeze swing by itself

Where am I? Oh the place to buy writing things
I have selected paper of light grey
the color of small decisions
black for the print
of my name and where to find me
I'd prefer another color except for the cost
I might as well go home They'll be needing food

It has been coming for me a long time
my name and what goes with it
Why do I have the impression
I just signed something I couldn't read in blood?

Spring Cleaning In A Lean Year

That spring the closets took hours
money was tight and getting tighter
getting rid of things had meant nothing
in the past but for who knew how long to come
nothing would replace them the way things were going
with money and not just in the family
just look at the thing selling the newspapers nowadays
The more she spent on the closets the more
she took things and their lack as something
she had to get rid of that spring
She packed the contents of the house then the house itself
and left them in a kingdom where manna grew in test tubes
the inhabitants could find nothing
but tears to express their thanks

The Priest And The Popsicle Man

Dee-dee-dah-dah
dee-dee-dah-dah
dee-dee-dah-dah
dum-dum

In summer sun the little white popsicle truck
rounds the block plinking its little white song
In the cool and quiet of his home
the priest thinks cool and quiet thoughts

Dee-dee-dah-dah
dee-dee-dah-dah
dee-dee-dah-dah
dum-dum

From the deep of her afternoon nap
the priest's child wakes and flies to the door
Daddy Daddy he's gone she wails
refusing to sleep again

Dee-dee-dah-dah
dee-dee-dah-dah
dee-dee-dah-dah
BANG

Deed done the priest returns his gun
to the silence of a bookshelf
At the window appears a dove
an olive branch grinning out the sides of its beak

Her Transfiguration

—for Jaimee

Gently she shakes out her apronful of children
Their giggle tumbles to the kitchen floor
falls into silence behind her while
she glides upstairs to her room

Up in her room she slips off her wedding ring
Her husband falls from mind as a man she never knew
When she slips off her clothes her past lovers number none
and her future lovers are men she does not miss

Palms turned up her hands slowly open
Her father stands in her right her mother in her left
and in their palms their parents
and in their parents' palms . . .

Till all questions bred in her flesh fade like genies
and her touch whitens all colors in her room
Down in the kitchen she finds her work done
by turning to do it

Through Kitchen Windows

Mornings the light without shines in
Evenings the light within shines out
The hand that feeds is at heart a wing

a day's flight ready to begin
The hand is a glass of milk enroute
Mornings the light without shines in

The hand is a wish to grab all things
and claim them with a toddler's shout
The hand that feeds is at heart a wing

The waking hand adjusts curtains
to make the world stay in and out
Mornings the light without shines in

The sleeping hand recalled famine
The dreaming hand recalled drought
The hand that feeds is at heart a wing

The hand holds to a light within
The hand learns to do without
Mornings the light without shines in
The hand that feeds is at heart a wing

April

The ground
is off and running
The trees
are off and running
Bud after bud takes off
into the sun the rain the sun
Three shades of green
compete for the edge of the freeway
Circling this house four pinks
leap ahead of the yellows
Seven days make seven worlds
The protectors of death
will lose their names
where winds collide
and the mountains
will pour themselves out

Primary Colors

A little girl in a blue dress looks
at herself in a picture
in her house

which is in something called a city
marked by a pin on a map
almost as big as she is
One of the big people
placed the pin
saying Look
this is where we live

Now she is in a big room
with mostly little people
whose we she has never met
whose number is higher than she can count
It is called school here
the nice lady called
the teacher
hands her paper and paint
Sky isn't yellow and grass isn't red
laughs the boy beside her into her picture
The little girl lifts her chin as high as she must
to keep the tears behind her eyes
The door she came in
opens back out
to the longest hall she has ever seen

From the front hall of her house a woman looks
at her little child going to school
Her right hand waves
to whatever his yellows and reds will be
On her left a wedding band gleams its partial clue

to the meaning of we

whose map she cannot read for its pinholes
whose calling she comprehends less
and less as she hears it
more and more
through her walls
which are slabs of blue air

Working Together: A Dream

Just the two of them
His eyes smile gold bars at her
Each time she suggests opening a window
he gives her a pay raise

A surgeon pads in
mask jacket instruments
He has flown three thousand miles
on a reddening maple leaf

With empty hands he covers her eyes
Through an open window sweet burn of leaves
Eyeless now she smiles at the man
who gives her a pay raise

Aging: From A Dream

In the corner of land where the dream was
nothing would do
The woods were a small uprising
compared to these
The trees were all losing their leaves
to a weaving of holes
What I saw in those woods I had lived in
was what I saw through
Your face my long time friend
was the face of a child
I watched you glide past like a harp
You had grown too young to know me

Ideal Love: From A Dream

In this rowboat it is early summer
water lilies let us drift only so far
we stroke one another and sometimes mention our love
in the still which holds us together we'll never need oars
Let's say the scene changed and the lake lay clear of lilies
and we had all the oars anyone could hope for
in what direction could we two possibly row?

For A Kinsman

Rain
it is raining again

The room fills with ancestors
yours and mine
They all look alike

When our eyes meet
the ancestors begin shouting and packing their tents
They tramp the line of our gaze
as though we owed them a path out of the desert

I watch the sweet light from your face
till I have stared some of them down
and the rest are quiet for now
and the water blurs their footprints
and I can feel the bleaching of our skin
here in the last corner of our last homeland
where each of us enters and enters the rain

Skyscape

—in memory of Ian

First a small
grey-brown bird
on the grey-brown
of the neighbors'
rooftop

Then the neighbors'
neighbors' rooftops
None as high as
the sway of greens
between them

Then from out of
the trees the jut
of a building
built suddenly
the sudden
shelter of a grey
haired man in
a brown suit
in a grey suit
in a brown suit
from the time his
hair was brown
till his love of
wings exploded
leaving
the neighbors
an interruption
jutting into view

Sing me your name
small bird
in a green wind
Sing me that
common name
I must
already know

The Last Few Tiles

Out the back of my eye she falls
a piece at a time
as tiles fall from an old mosaic:

sunbeams on a bowl of oranges
a closetful of glass slippers
a front door open to the thought of summer

Her latest heart-throb
races in pieces around his madness
her latest always outruns the one before him:

months ago she left her radio here
I don't dare turn it on

May

Where the leaf expands to its full shape
where the spore tassel drops the seed
see how the year falls in place

Where the eye grows used to early dawns
where the hand lifts the weight of the bloom
see how the wide light is born

Where balance finds the angles of the calf
where depth fills the coat of the lamb
steadily the young year stands

To A Childhood Friend

In the long space
since your last letter
the rest of your family appears

Old enough to be his own father
your father dies
war horses charging across his brow
his chin a sunflower
still tilting to the light
Your mother putters in the flowerbeds
by the large house
All its whiteness is hers now
She wishes the mourners
would leave her to her violets
Next door your older sister
makes things safe for the children
she imagines in her children
Miles north your younger sister
keeps to her rows of vegetables

Perhaps this family is not exactly yours
or perhaps your last sporadic letters
were written by not exactly you
and I will not exactly
hear from you again

Mountain Road

Farmhouse and fields
wildflowers
cows
PRIMITIVE ROAD NO WARNING SIGNS
cows
wildflowers
farmhouse and fields
same as before
Pavement ends
woods deepen
one lane road
climbs
Now we see what we saw
a few miles back:
PRIMITIVE ROAD NO WARNING SIGNS
in after-image
vivid and black
Road narrows
road climbs
dust rises
dust on windows
first day of summer
sun through trees
When the woods don't
line the road
nothing
lines the road
 Bend in road
log in road
we round the bend
PRIMITIVE ROAD NO WARNING SIGNS
flares like a tombstone
in my mind's eye
Woods thin out
sky widens
almost the top
almost the end
of the ride
Snow flung
across the road

we open the dusty doors
and climb to the top

The wind strolls round and round in its inner chambers
scattered pines radiate perfection of green
flowers flare like bits of prism
and the sky is a blue well
The life I cling to is a chip of loose rock
sliding without sound through the sound of wind
Clinging to me is love for the man and boy I walk with
love begging Love for its home in the sea

Early Morning Mist

In the mist the grass stands alone
the poplar stands alone
dogwood cherry fir
the house and the house beside the house
alone and nothing even whispers to anything else

In the mist the world enters its first day
the white rabbit has always been three months old
the tomatoes have always been ripe
the petunias dead
the newspaper is a stage prop on the porch

Here is the school bus
I see a small boy in a back seat
I see a small boy find him and he is my son
immersing himself in the number two in the lurching bus
the bus has left

the mist has left
I stand eye to eye
with the number two
its tribe of successors
nomads

Porch Poem

I dreamt my ninety year old neighbor died
a stereo on his porch was my clue
left on all night the record spun like wild
my breath spun in my chest from what I knew
Waking to view his house I feared my fear
his blinds also were raised to greet the day
his empty porch seemed somehow too near
my lack of ease was left with nothing to say

Why fear for a life still offering aplomb
at ninety years in handshake dress and speech?
On my porch the mailman leaves a bomb
whose picture stares out from a magazine
the picture glares in orange gone berserk
Trying to fear an old man's death won't work.

By The Time I Am Ready To Fish

An army of firs divides
the sun jumps back
in its own face
where this water takes over
like so many miles of thunder

My seven year old casts out
reels in
and wins
tall
within his laughter

My husband
makes use of a line
he loses sight of
bit by bit lets fly his whole smallness
into the milk blue rush

By the time I am ready to fish
the spinner of my birth my death
and what gleams between
is tumbling down river
with an occasional tree

Pause In The Weather

When the empire of ice dissolved here
what stays green took charge
and the weather paused

then came the fingers
which could build fires
in the damp of the forest

To inherit the embers
the coming of more fingers
some bringing the invention

of the match
and questioning the sky
which kept turning its back

The match flares
and the weather continues
to make no commitments but

while my tea cools rapidly in its cup
let me start over at the point
where fir and fog meet

September

The North is coming
See it in the park
where it trails the geese
landing at dusk
for one night only
to peck at the ground
to gulp and peck

The earth retreats
to the earth
the sun to the sun
Everything is going home
and wisdom is upon us
heavy as tomatoes
ripe on the vine

The marigolds blare:
it is time to bow to the rain
it is time to open the cedar chest
fresh as your grief may be

In The Distant Listener's Ear

—for Richard Eberhart

In the scent of apple blossoms you are born
At the entrance to the quarry you are born
Out of the cries of ospreys you are borne

Before day abandons dawn you are born
In the precision of spiders you are born
In the scent of apple blossoms you are born

In the light at the edge of light you are born
In the air between your words you are born
Out of the cries of ospreys you are borne

In the helplessness of Eve you are born
In the helplessness of Adam you are born
In the scent of apple blossoms you are born

After the deafness after the bomb you are born
In the distant listener's ear you are born
Out of the cries of ospreys you are borne

In the expected dusk you are born
In the unexpected death you are born
In the scent of apple blossoms you are born
Out of the cries of ospreys you are borne

Flying South

Two or three leaves
give up a silent amen
After this we open our ears

The dusk seats itself among us
while we eat peaches
The dusk

which is a memory of peaches
a flock of birds flown south in some other year

Each of us finds it gone at a different time
that same flock

risen from the hand we hold back
flown from a season each hears alone
till we hear one another hearing the same
amen

Then
from the south
the sound
of an unlocked gate

Mailslot

The slip of possibilities
The flap claps shut
The mailman scurries away
He has been replaced again
He has stuffed the box tighter
There is less to read than yesterday
The gloss on paper heightens

Remember His gift of fish
and later the drawings
of fish in the sand?
They were word enough then
weren't they?

It is tomorrow and the mail has come.
Remember that substance called sand?
Will someone try with me
to find sand?

Basement

Turn on the light
hold the stair rail
Step down
a step at a time
Here is the floor
that does not give
Here the old stacks
of old news
What was it you
were looking for
that must be here
if it's anywhere
The right wrench
that's what
Turn on the light
at the workbench
Someday you will
organize this mess
of nails and rags
Someday you'll find
what you're looking for
when you come down here
and poke through cupboards
of pale paints in unopened cans
left by the residents before last:
can you see the mattress you left leaning against the furnace?
Who lives here next will pick up your bed and walk with it.
Here is the basement. All you can do is pray.

yer Of My Thirty-Fifth Winter

A flower garden from my first summers
runs on and on this evening
The sky careens with fireflies
as it did then

What's changed is the garden blooming into a prayer
the fireflies increasing in number
their light becoming permanent

The Woman In The Woods

She built her house of rock
using stones from a river
deep in the woods
She lived autumn to autumn
harvesting stones and building walls
while the woods called:
this is home
you and the gold coins
which flicker in October's dress
are one and the same

Autumn by autumn Stone by stone
she built a house nothing could shake
And when the thing came
which shook down the house
she was left to the tumbling hands of the river
she was left to the hollows of her hands
and the caches of squirrels
When the stones return
she told herself
I'll build a house of rock

After a year the stones return
By now she is weaving willow sprigs
The stones fill the woods
like the first snow of winter
The flex of her fingers
and the flex of willow
are one and the same
Goodbye she tells the stones
I've learned how to live in a basket
and a basket is what I prefer

Touching The Moss

The river escapes
what remains is the life spreading back from its banks
Drops of light make silver of the alders
standing with their rough brothers the cedars
among tiny white flowers
and arcs of fern

Gone again

Touching the moss
won't bring home the river
which even while slipping beside us
must be glimpsed in retrospect if at all
An instance of silver light
leaving

October

Nights line up
with a drummer in the lead
Dawns we hear him beating time
on the other side of the hill

Days are the beating
of a drum coming close
Each day is a drum and the drum is a heart
on the other side of the hill

Days are the rains parading home
They are the flash of leaves
leaving one by one
leaving us on the other side

where an old woman lights a bonfire
and greets us one by one by name
strangers each to the next
listening for drumbeats

The Goal

Sometimes the goal is a horse
bearing us to a mountaintop
where the ice melts

Where the ice melts flows a horse we can't mount
We know where it lives by the heat of our palms
when it nuzzles for food

Sometimes the goal is a valley
where a horse forever grazes and drinks
When we wander that valley our hands refuse to feed us

Today

Today hasn't been here all day
Word of its return
fails to arrive
over and over by phone
The rabbit in the basement
attacks an empty suitcase
An hour shifts slightly in its sleep
Dust falls but not on the mirrors
If only today would leave instructions for its absence
but it's older than the number one
and not given to change

Sticks Equation

One stick equals a blind man
two sticks equal a flame
three sticks equal a promised land

and four the sound of our names
five equal an infant's toes
six equal nothing plus rain

seven equal a perfect rose
eight an eight-lane highway
nine a dragon in repose

Fresh sticks on the ground today
walk with care while walk we may

Day After The End Of Days

Those chosen
to survive
pitch tents
in a maze
of gleaming girders
It is November
the tulips bloom
It is July
An old woman
mumbles how
when she was a girl
the tulips
bloomed in spring
Some say she
has grown confused
Others
in the dark
of their blood
feel a tremor
of seasons
For this feeling
they have no name
They pocket the dust
of broken bricks
and carry it
to what water
they find
Into the water
they pour the dust
and cry O Creator
Out of this clay
create us

Messages From The Moon

I.   I have turned my back

Now when you look for me
you see the surfaces of leaves
but not the leaves themselves

When listening you hear
the words of men
but not their voices
and the protest of children
walking up taller
less convinced
of owning the trees

Till I turn again
be still
or you will drift
in the crosswind of women
who would be mothers
but not have them
You will fall
into everything
that's missing

II.   Now I show half my face

A child who was deaf
wants to hear your song
When he turns your way
listen to me and sing
what I sing you
He will hear his voice

A deaf old woman
wants to steal new ears
When she turns your way
turn my way and weep
Quiet the song
which I sing you
for the child

I will reflect you
in the light you need

Walk where light meets earth
when you hear my footsteps
When hearing all else turn yours
to the shadows of leaves

III.   Tonight I meet everything
eye to eye

When looking at the trees
you see the trembling of roots
When listening you hear
the voices of women
and the muteness of women
whose words have no voice

Turn to the man you need
Listen to me and tell him
what I tell you
He hears the fullness
I bring to your tone
You hear all words which
have lost their voices
Tonight they run the fields
for a tree to hide behind

And from the ground
on which you stand
breaks forth laughter

IV.   Now I hide half my face

A crow calls your name
from the top of a tree
so tall that although
you climb all night
the sound of the crow

persists from above
as though you
had created the black sky

At dawn you see
you are halfway up
and the next branch
would be too thin
for your weight

This point where
your climb must end
is the home of four doves
Through the call of the crow
I have brought you to the doves
Be here when I turn my back

November

Marching
into the sky
a poplar halts
Its brass instruments
fall silent falling
the long distance
to earth
which says nothing
but receives
the autumn leaves
like any other
multitude losing
its music
In the space where
the leaves had hung
where the snow
will whirl
a hush moves in
At its heart sits
a bird
sitting on eggs
we'll never see
but must believe in
branching as we do
into the trackless
thin light

A Way Through

Start with a rose
close your eyes
turn around
walk
When you feel the path reach the edge of a cliff
open your eyes and see the star
where the rose began

Start with a star
close your eyes
turn around
walk
When you feel the path reach the end of the sky
opcn your cycs and scc thc void
where the star began

Start with a void
close your eyes
turn around
walk
When you feel a path beneath your feet
open your eyes and see the rose
awaiting you all this time

Close your eyes
turn around
walk

Hermit

—after a painting by Stephen Lowe

His left
faces this way

ahead of him
maybe snow or fog
behind him
fog or snow
maybe a driving rain

behind him
a wash of brown and red
a tangle of thin
dark trees
above him
a wash of brown leaves
about to fall

the foot he lifts
leads him out of the trees
into a white blur

on the detail which is the hermit
a red robe

patches of leaf-strewn earth
shift forward
to meet the eye

Captors And Captives

One rainy day the eagles were taken captive
One rainy day the grounded captors lost their way
One rainy day the sky had no more wings to give

Whose fault is this cried the captors each holding a sieve
to the sky in the hope of feathers gone astray
One rainy day the eagles were taken captive

Without flight of eagles in what can we believe
the captors cried again to the source of the rain
One rainy day the sky had no more wings to give

The rain falling on and on brought nothing to retrieve
neither talons nor a path of flight nor strength
One rainy day the eagles were taken captive

And gradually the ground refused to receive
the death of whatever had reached its dying day
One rainy day the sky had no more wings to give

Then the captors that they might continue to live
led two wounded eagles to sky male and female
One rainy day the eagles were taken captive
One rainy day the sky had no more wings to give

Flag

When a flag goes up
whatever it stands for
clicks into place
at the top of a pole
then plummets as a bird
dying in sunlight
The least breeze
will cause this death
for the wind lifts flags
from the colors and patterns
of the wingless
A flag
bears allegiance to wind
a flag is the wind regaled
When a flag falls
when a day folds
and the notes of its bugles
lie closed as stones
history boards its slow boats
sets sail again for home

Directions

North is a dream
Of heat
Rocks covered with ice
Tell of this dream which turns white
Hitting the air

South is a dream
Of rain on leaves
Under sun-beaten rocks
The hunger of lizards
Holds its ground

East is a dream of answers
All questions moving inside it
Settle as sunsets
Throughout old cities at peace

West
Entrance to dreams
See how every direction
Turns your way

After A Storm

Now the sky is alone and still
The battered grass rises to its feet
The morning wanders the hills as a cat
drawing its destination from its toes

Yesterday splinters and blows out to sea
Tomorrow is an ark
we built when we weren't looking
Today is our footsteps running like prophets to find us

Blossom Shock

Caught
by this earlier sunrise

cherry blossoms
the exact moment of death has come and gone

what winter buries grows harder to name
each spring there is more of it

each time the trees repeat themselves
its cry for a name grows louder in our bones

The Habit Of Missing

When we no longer miss
what we missed for so long
we had given what was missing its own room
What remains is a habit
of missing
and we notice the habit
for the first time

We awake to help it dress
in our best clothes
At breakfast
it tastes with our tongues
gazes out the window through our eyes

On our feet it rises
having eaten with us so often
we take it for ourselves walking
walking
entering a room we no longer use
A room of echoes which for the first time
we don't hear

Living With It

Wherever I go It turns out a light
I've grown used to turning
from where I'm going to
where the dark just fell
leaving me in the only
home I've known
which falls
light by light
into the rising flowers

Marjorie Power was born in 1947 and raised in Stamford, Connecticut. She is a graduate of Abbot Academy in Andover, Massachusetts and San Francisco State College. Since 1970, she has lived in Seattle. She is married and has a nine year old son.